AIR FRYER DELIGHT

QUICK AND HEALTHY RECIPES

VIOLETA T. HODGE

Copyright © 2023 VIOLETE T. HODGE

All right reserved. No part of this publication may be reproduced, distributed, or transmitted in any form or by any means, including photocopying, recording, or other electronic or mechanical methods, without the prior written permission of the publisher, except in the case of brief quotation embodied in critical reviews and certain other noncommercial uses permitted by copyright law.

Table of Contents

Introduction to Air Frying 5

GETTING STARTED WITH YOUR AIR FRYER 7

BREAKFAST BITES AND BRUNCH BLISS 11

APPETIZERS & SNACK ATTACK 15

POULTRY PERFECTION: CHICKEN AND TURKEY DISHES 20

SEAFOOD SENSATIONS: FISH AND SEAFOOD RECIPES 25

MEAT MARVELS: PORK AND BEEF DELIGHTS 30

VEGGIE VIBES: VEGETARIAN AIR FRYER CREATIONS 35

SIDES AND SMALL PLATES 40

QUICK AND HEALTHY DESSERTS 45

AIR FRYER BAKING: CAKES, PASTRIES, AND MORE 50

SALADS WITH A CRUNCH 55

GLOBAL FLAVORS: AIR-FRIED INTERNATIONAL CUISINE 60

HEALTHY EATING ON A BUDGET 65

30-MINUTE MEALS WITH YOUR AIR FRYER 70

LOW-CARB AND KETO-FRIENDLY OPTIONS 75

AIR FRYER TIPS AKND TRICKS 80

ENTERTAINING WITH YOUR AIR FRYER 85

FAMILY-FRIENDLY FAVORITES 90

SWEET ENDINGS: DELECTABLE DESSERT CREATIONS 95

INTRODUCTION TO AIR FRYING

Welcome to the world of air frying, where you'll discover a revolutionary way to cook delicious, quick, and healthy meals. If you've just acquired an air fryer or have been using one for a while, this cookbook is your passport to culinary exploration and nutritious indulgence.

Air frying has taken the culinary world by storm, offering a guilt-free approach to enjoying your favorite dishes. With its ability to mimic the satisfying crunch of deep-frying while using significantly less oil, the air fryer has become a kitchen essential for those seeking a healthier lifestyle without sacrificing flavor.

In this cookbook, we will embark on a flavorful journey through a diverse collection of recipes that showcase the versatility of the air fryer. From breakfast to dessert, and everything in between, you'll find a wide range of recipes that are not only quick and easy but also designed with your well-being in mind. We've crafted each recipe to strike a perfect balance between convenience, taste, and health.

Our goal is simple: to provide you with a culinary adventure that delights your taste buds, nourishes your body, and simplifies your time in the kitchen. Whether you're a seasoned air fryer enthusiast or a newcomer to this innovative cooking method, you'll find inspiration within these pages to create wholesome meals that will satisfy your cravings and impress your loved ones.

So, let's embark on this journey together and uncover the joys of air frying. Get ready to enjoy

"Air Fryer Delights" and experience the magic of cooking quick, healthy, and delectable dishes that will leave you craving for more.

GETTING STARTED WITH YOUR AIR FRYER

Before you dive into the delicious world of air frying, it's essential to familiarize yourself with your trusty kitchen companion – the air fryer. This chapter will guide you through everything you need to know to make the most of your air fryer and ensure your cooking experience is both safe and successful.

Choosing the Right Air Fryer:

In this section, we'll explore the different types and sizes of air fryers available in the market. We'll help you choose the one that best suits your needs and kitchen space. Whether you have a countertop model or a built-in air fryer, we've got you covered.

Understanding Your Air Fryer:

It's important to get acquainted with the various components and settings of your air fryer. We'll break down the parts of an air fryer, such as the basket, the heating element, and the control panel. You'll learn how to preheat your air fryer, set the cooking temperature, and adjust the cooking time.

Essential Accessories:

Discover the accessories that can enhance your air frying experience. From grill pans to baking dishes, these tools can help you expand your cooking repertoire and make your air fryer even more versatile.

Cooking Tips and Techniques:

To achieve the best results, we'll share essential air frying tips and techniques. You'll learn about the right oil to use, how to prevent food from sticking, and how to achieve that perfect crispy texture. We'll also cover safety precautions to ensure worry-free cooking.

Maintenance and Cleaning:

Keeping your air fryer in top condition is crucial. We'll provide guidance on how to clean and maintain your appliance for longevity and optimum performance.

Troubleshooting Common Issues:

If you encounter any problems while using your air fryer, this section will help you troubleshoot and resolve common issues, ensuring that your air frying journey remains stress-free.

With this chapter as your guide, you'll be fully equipped to get the most out of your air fryer and embark on a successful cooking adventure. So, let's start this culinary journey together!

BREAKFAST BITES AND BRUNCH BLISS

There's no better way to start your day than with a delicious and satisfying breakfast. In this chapter, we'll explore a variety of breakfast and brunch recipes that you can prepare in your air fryer. From quick weekday breakfast bites to leisurely weekend brunch indulgences, you'll find options to suit every morning mood.

- **Classic Bacon and Egg Sandwich:**

Experience the perfect combination of crispy bacon, perfectly cooked eggs, and a warm, toasted bun, all prepared in your air fryer.

- **French Toast Sticks:**

Enjoy the sweet and comforting taste of French toast, transformed into convenient and dippable sticks.

- **Veggie-Filled Omelets:**

Create custom omelets with your favorite vegetables, cheese, and herbs, all cooked to fluffy perfection.

- **Cinnamon Roll Twists:**

Indulge in the irresistible aroma and flavor of cinnamon rolls, but with a fun twist that's easy to make.

- **Breakfast Potatoes:**

Crispy and seasoned to perfection, these air-fried potatoes make an ideal side dish or a hearty breakfast option.

- **Blueberry Pancake Bites:**

Tiny pockets of fluffy pancake goodness filled with juicy blueberries, perfect for on-the-go mornings.

- **Sausage and Egg Breakfast Burritos:**

Wrap up savory sausage, scrambled eggs, and cheese in a tortilla for a satisfying breakfast to start your day.

- **Avocado Toast with a Crunch:**

Elevate your avocado toast game with a crispy twist, adding a delightful crunch to this trendy classic.

- **Belgian Waffles with Berries:**

Experience the joy of Belgian waffles with a golden, crispy exterior and a fluffy, tender interior, topped with fresh berries.

- **Quiche Lorraine:**

A classic quiche filled with savory ham, cheese, and a delicate custard, all baked to perfection in your air fryer.

- **Breakfast Quesadillas:**

Combine scrambled eggs, cheese, and your favorite ingredients in a quesadilla that's both satisfying and portable.

- **Nutty Granola and Yogurt Parfait:**

Craft a healthy and hearty granola parfait with your favorite nuts, fruits, and yogurt.

Whether you're in the mood for a quick weekday breakfast or a leisurely brunch with friends and family, this chapter offers a delightful array of recipes that will satisfy your morning cravings and make every breakfast a memorable experience.

APPETIZERS & SNACK ATTACK

This chapter is dedicated to those moments when you crave something delicious to nibble on, whether you're hosting a party, enjoying a movie night, or simply looking for a quick and satisfying bite. With your air fryer, you can whip up a wide range of appetizers and snacks that will satisfy your taste buds and keep your guests coming back for more.

- **Crispy Mozzarella Sticks:**

Experience the perfect combination of crunchy coating and gooey cheese, served with a zesty marinara sauce for dipping.

- **Loaded Potato Skins:**

Transform potatoes into crispy, loaded vessels of flavor, topped with cheese, bacon, and sour cream.

- **Buffalo Cauliflower Bites:**

Spicy and satisfying, these air-fried cauliflower bites are perfect for game day or as a spicy snack.

- **Spinach and Artichoke Dip:**

A creamy and cheesy dip that's a party favorite, served with toasted bread or veggie sticks.

- **Stuffed Mushrooms:**

Delight in mushroom caps stuffed with flavorful fillings and air-fried to perfection.

- **Sweet Potato Fries:**

Create crispy, seasoned sweet potato fries that are both delicious and nutritious.

- **Chicken Wings Three Ways:**

Explore the world of chicken wings with three mouthwatering recipes, from classic hot wings to sweet and savory flavors.

- **Zucchini Chips:**

Make light and crispy zucchini chips as a healthy alternative to traditional potato chips.

- **Spicy Jalapeño Poppers:**

Fire up your taste buds with jalapeño poppers filled with cream cheese and wrapped in bacon.

- **Homemade Onion Rings:**

Experience the satisfying crunch of homemade onion rings without the deep frying.

- **Salsa and Guacamole:**

Prepare fresh and flavorful dips for your tortilla chips, ready in a breeze.

- **Asian-inspired Spring Rolls:**

Roll up a variety of fresh ingredients in rice paper and serve with a dipping sauce for a light and satisfying snack.

- **Crispy Chickpeas:**

Create seasoned, crunchy chickpeas for a protein-packed and addictive snack.

- **Air-Fried Mini Meatballs:**

Perfectly bite-sized and packed with flavor, these mini meatballs are great for parties or as a snack.

- **Loaded Nachos:**

Layer crispy tortilla chips with cheese, beans, jalapeños, and other toppings, all cooked to cheesy perfection.

Whether you're entertaining guests or simply enjoying a quiet night in, these air fryer appetizers and snacks are sure to satisfy your cravings. Get ready for a snacking adventure that's both delicious and hassle-free.

POULTRY PERFECTION: CHICKEN AND TURKEY DISHES

In this chapter, we'll explore the world of poultry prepared to crispy perfection in your air fryer. Chicken and turkey are incredibly versatile, and your air fryer can bring out their best flavors and textures. From classic favorites to creative innovations, these recipes will make poultry dishes the stars of your meals.

- **Classic Fried Chicken:**

Achieve that famous crispy coating and juicy interior with less oil, making this a healthier version of a beloved classic.

- **Lemon Herb Roast Chicken:**

Infuse your roast chicken with zesty lemon and aromatic herbs for a delectable and fragrant main dish.

- **Honey Mustard Glazed Turkey Wings:**

Enjoy tender turkey wings with a sweet and tangy glaze that's perfect for snacking or as a main course.

- **Chicken Parmesan:**

A lighter take on this Italian favorite, with crispy chicken cutlets topped with marinara sauce and melted cheese.

- **Garlic Butter Turkey Breast:**

Savor a succulent turkey breast with garlic butter, ensuring every bite is flavorful and tender.

- **BBQ Chicken Drumsticks:**

Indulge in the smoky and sweet flavors of barbecue chicken drumsticks that are finger-licking good.

- **Teriyaki Chicken Thighs:**

Create a savory and slightly sweet teriyaki glaze for tender and flavorful chicken thighs.

- **Chicken Tenders with Dipping Sauces:**

Perfectly crispy chicken tenders served with an array of dipping sauces for a fun and satisfying meal.

- **Lemon Pepper Turkey Cutlets:**

Elevate turkey cutlets with zesty lemon and bold pepper flavors for a delightful and easy dish.

- **Spicy Buffalo Chicken Tenders:**

Fire up your taste buds with spicy buffalo chicken tenders that are perfect for game day or any day.

- **Tandoori Chicken Skewers:**

Experience the vibrant and aromatic flavors of tandoori chicken skewers, marinated to perfection.

- **Herb-Crusted Turkey Cutlets:**

Coat turkey cutlets in a delightful herb crust for a fresh and flavorful twist on poultry.

- **Chicken and Vegetable Stir-Fry:**

Create a quick and healthy stir-fry with tender chicken and a medley of colorful vegetables.

- **Panko-Crusted Turkey Burgers:**

Satisfy your burger cravings with juicy and crispy turkey patties coated in panko breadcrumbs.

- **Chicken Alfredo Stuffed Peppers:**

Transform classic stuffed peppers by filling them with a creamy chicken Alfredo mixture.

From the simplicity of crispy chicken tenders to the sophistication of herb-infused turkey dishes, this chapter is your gateway to poultry perfection. Your air fryer will be your trusty sidekick in creating these mouthwatering chicken and turkey recipes.

SEAFOOD SENSATIONS: FISH AND SEAFOOD RECIPES

This chapter is a deep dive into the world of fish and seafood, all brought to life with the magic of your air fryer. Whether you're a seafood enthusiast or just looking to incorporate more fish into your diet, these recipes will have you hooked. From delicate fillets to succulent shrimp, we've got it all.

- **Crispy Lemon Garlic Shrimp:**

Delight in succulent shrimp coated in a crispy, lemon-infused batter that bursts with flavor.

- **Parmesan-Crusted Tilapia:**

Transform tilapia into a gourmet experience with a cheesy and crispy Parmesan crust.

- **Spicy Cajun Catfish:**

Create a zesty Cajun seasoning for catfish fillets that will transport your taste buds to the bayou.

- **Coconut-Crusted Mahi-Mahi:**

Experience the tropical taste of coconut-crusted mahi-mahi with a sweet and savory dipping sauce.

- **Scallops with Garlic Butter:**

Savor perfectly seared scallops drizzled in a garlicky butter sauce, a true seafood delicacy.

- **Baked Salmon with Herbs:**

Cook salmon fillets to tender perfection with a medley of aromatic herbs and spices.

- **Tuna Steaks with Wasabi Aioli:**

Spice up your tuna steaks with a zesty wasabi aioli that complements their rich flavor.

- **Mediterranean-Style Grilled Swordfish:**

Infuse swordfish steaks with Mediterranean flavors, featuring olives, tomatoes, and herbs.

- **Crispy Coconut Shrimp:**

Enjoy a tropical twist on a classic favorite with crispy coconut-coated shrimp and a fruity dipping sauce.

- **Lemon Dill Cod Fillets:**

Elevate cod fillets with the bright and refreshing flavors of lemon and dill for a light and flavorful dish.

- **Teriyaki Glazed Salmon Bowls:**

Serve air-fried salmon atop a bed of rice with teriyaki glaze and fresh vegetables for a complete meal.

- **Garlic Butter Prawns:**

Indulge in garlic-infused butter prawns that are rich, flavorful, and incredibly easy to prepare.

- **Blackened Red Snapper:**

Create a blackened spice rub for red snapper fillets that packs a punch of flavor and heat.

- **Seafood Tacos:**

Prepare flavorful seafood fillings for tacos, from shrimp to fish, complete with fresh toppings.

- **Shrimp and Broccoli Stir-Fry:**

Whip up a quick and healthy stir-fry with plump shrimp, crisp broccoli, and a savory sauce.

These seafood recipes are designed to highlight the natural flavors of fish and shellfish while making the most of your air fryer's capabilities. Get ready to explore a world of seafood sensations that will leave your taste buds yearning for more.

MEAT MARVELS: PORK AND BEEF DELIGHTS

In this chapter, we're diving into the realm of pork and beef dishes, showcasing the rich and savory flavors of these meats when prepared to perfection in your air fryer. From succulent steaks to tender pork chops, these recipes will satisfy your carnivorous cravings and elevate your dinner table.

- **Perfectly Seared Ribeye Steak:**

Achieve a mouthwatering, restaurant-quality sear on your ribeye steak, complemented by your favorite seasonings.

- **Honey Glazed Pork Tenderloin:**

Indulge in juicy and sweet glazed pork tenderloin with a hint of honey and spices.

- **BBQ Pulled Pork Sliders:**

Create tender pulled pork sliders with smoky barbecue flavor, served with your favorite coleslaw.

- **Crispy Pork Belly Bites:**

Savor the irresistible crunch and rich flavors of air-fried pork belly bites.

- **Beef and Broccoli Stir-Fry:**

Whip up a quick and flavorful stir-fry featuring thinly sliced beef, crisp broccoli, and a savory sauce.

- **Stuffed Bell Peppers with Ground Beef:**

Fill bell peppers with a hearty mixture of ground beef, rice, and tomatoes, all cooked to perfection.

- **Garlic Herb Pork Chops:**

Enjoy flavorful and juicy pork chops infused with garlic and aromatic herbs.

- **Crispy Beef Tacos:**

Prepare crispy taco shells filled with seasoned ground beef and your favorite toppings.

- **Teriyaki Pork Kabobs:**

Skewer tender pork pieces with colorful vegetables and a savory teriyaki glaze for a delightful meal.

- **Spicy Sausage Stuffed Mushrooms:**

Combine spicy sausage with mushroom caps for a delectable and savory appetizer.

- **Beef and Black Bean Quesadillas:**

Craft quesadillas filled with seasoned beef, black beans, and cheese for a satisfying and cheesy treat.

- **Italian-Style Pork Roast:**

Create an Italian-inspired pork roast with fragrant herbs, tomatoes, and a hint of garlic.

- **Meatloaf Muffins:**

Prepare individual-sized meatloaf muffins, each bursting with flavor and a savory glaze.

- **Sweet and Sour Pork:**

Whip up a tangy and sweet sauce for crispy air-fried pork chunks, served with bell peppers and pineapple.

- **Smoky Chili with Ground Beef:**

Make a rich and smoky chili with ground beef, beans, and a blend of spices for a hearty and warming dish.

VEGGIE VIBES: VEGETARIAN AIR FRYER CREATIONS

This chapter celebrates the vibrant and diverse world of vegetarian cuisine, all prepared to perfection in your air fryer. Whether you're a dedicated vegetarian or simply looking to add more plant-based dishes to your diet, these recipes will introduce you to a world of meatless delights.

- **Crispy Vegetable Spring Rolls:**

Indulge in perfectly crispy spring rolls filled with a medley of fresh vegetables and served with a sweet dipping sauce.

- **Stuffed Bell Peppers with Quinoa:**

Create stuffed bell peppers filled with protein-packed quinoa, vegetables, and a flavorful tomato sauce.

- **Sweet Potato Fries with Dipping Sauces:**

Enjoy the delightful combination of sweet and savory with air-fried sweet potato fries and an array of dipping sauces.

- **Vegetarian Stuffed Mushrooms:**

Savor stuffed mushroom caps filled with a savory mixture of cheese, herbs, and breadcrumbs.

- **Eggplant Parmesan:**

Experience the Italian classic with crispy air-fried eggplant slices layered with marinara sauce and melted cheese.

- **Spinach and Feta Stuffed Portobello Mushrooms:**

Delight in large Portobello mushrooms filled with a creamy spinach and feta mixture.

- **Crispy Tofu Bites:**

Transform tofu into crunchy, bite-sized morsels, perfect for snacking or as a protein-packed addition to salads.

- **Falafel Patties with Tahini Sauce:**

Prepare crispy falafel patties served with a creamy tahini sauce and warm pita bread.

- **Air-Fried Veggie Tempura:**

Enjoy light and crispy vegetable tempura, featuring a variety of colorful veggies and a flavorful dipping sauce.

- **Caprese Stuffed Avocado:**

Combine ripe avocados with fresh mozzarella, tomatoes, and basil for a refreshing and satisfying dish.

- **Veggie Quesadillas:**

Craft quesadillas filled with a mix of sautéed vegetables, cheese, and your favorite seasonings.

- **Crispy Brussels Sprouts:**

Turn Brussels sprouts into crispy bites of perfection, seasoned to your liking.

- **Sweet and Spicy Air-Fried Cauliflower:**

Experience the balance of sweet and spicy flavors with air-fried cauliflower florets.

- **Spinach and Mushroom Quiche:**

Create a delightful quiche filled with sautéed spinach, mushrooms, and cheese in a golden crust.

- **Ratatouille:**

Prepare the classic French dish with layers of beautifully arranged vegetables, cooked to tender perfection.

SIDES AND SMALL PLATES

Side dishes and small plates have the power to elevate any meal, whether they accompany a main course or stand on their own. In this chapter, you'll discover a tempting array of small bites and sides that can be prepared quickly and easily in your air fryer.

- **Garlic Parmesan Potato Wedges:**

Indulge in crispy potato wedges seasoned with garlic and Parmesan, served with a creamy dipping sauce.

- **Crispy Zucchini Fritters:**

Whip up golden and crunchy zucchini fritters, perfect as a snack or side dish.

- **Onion Rings with Spicy Aioli:**

Enjoy the delightful crunch of air-fried onion rings paired with a zesty and spicy aioli.

- **Roasted Brussels Sprouts with Balsamic Glaze:**

Experience the perfect blend of roasted Brussels sprouts with a drizzle of balsamic glaze.

- **Caprese Salad Skewers:**

Create bite-sized caprese skewers featuring mozzarella, cherry tomatoes, and basil, drizzled with balsamic reduction.

- **Air-Fried Garlic Mushrooms:**

Savor the rich and earthy flavor of garlic-seasoned mushrooms, air-fried to perfection.

- **Truffle Parmesan Fries:**

Elevate your fries with the indulgent combination of truffle oil and Parmesan cheese.

- **Pita Bread Chips with Hummus:**

Prepare crispy pita bread chips served with creamy hummus, perfect for snacking.

- **Baked Avocado Fries:**

Experience the unique texture and flavor of avocado fries, served with a zesty dipping sauce.

- **Quinoa and Vegetable Stuffed Peppers:**

Create small stuffed peppers filled with a wholesome mixture of quinoa and colorful vegetables.

- **Cheesy Stuffed Mushrooms:**

Indulge in mushrooms filled with a creamy and cheesy mixture, perfectly air-fried for a satisfying side.

- **Crispy Polenta Bites:**

Turn polenta into delightful bites with a crispy exterior and a soft, creamy interior.

- **Mediterranean Mezze Platter:**

Assemble a colorful mezze platter with an assortment of small plates, including olives, feta, and stuffed grape leaves.

- **Sweet Potato Tots:**

Experience the sweet and crispy joy of sweet potato tots, perfect as a snack or side.

- **Spinach and Artichoke Dip Stuffed Peppers:**

Combine the flavors of spinach and artichoke dip with sweet bell peppers for a delectable small plate.

Whether you're hosting a party, looking for a quick snack, or seeking the perfect complement to your main course, these sides and small plates offer a variety of delicious options. Let your air fryer take the lead in creating these delightful additions to your meals.

QUICK AND HEALTHY DESSERTS

Side dishes and small plates have the power to elevate any meal, whether they accompany a main course or stand on their own. In this chapter, you'll discover a tempting array of small bites and sides that can be prepared quickly and easily in your air fryer.

- **Garlic Parmesan Potato Wedges:**

Indulge in crispy potato wedges seasoned with garlic and Parmesan, served with a creamy dipping sauce.

- **Crispy Zucchini Fritters:**

Whip up golden and crunchy zucchini fritters, perfect as a snack or side dish.

- **Onion Rings with Spicy Aioli:**

Enjoy the delightful crunch of air-fried onion rings paired with a zesty and spicy aioli.

- **Roasted Brussels Sprouts with Balsamic Glaze:**

Experience the perfect blend of roasted Brussels sprouts with a drizzle of balsamic glaze.

- **Caprese Salad Skewers:**

Create bite-sized caprese skewers featuring mozzarella, cherry tomatoes, and basil, drizzled with balsamic reduction.

- **Air-Fried Garlic Mushrooms:**

Savor the rich and earthy flavor of garlic-seasoned mushrooms, air-fried to perfection.

- **Truffle Parmesan Fries:**

Elevate your fries with the indulgent combination of truffle oil and Parmesan cheese.

- **Pita Bread Chips with Hummus:**

Prepare crispy pita bread chips served with creamy hummus, perfect for snacking.

- **Baked Avocado Fries:**

Experience the unique texture and flavor of avocado fries, served with a zesty dipping sauce.

- **Quinoa and Vegetable Stuffed Peppers:**

Create small stuffed peppers filled with a wholesome mixture of quinoa and colorful vegetables.

- **Cheesy Stuffed Mushrooms:**

Indulge in mushrooms filled with a creamy and cheesy mixture, perfectly air-fried for a satisfying side.

- **Crispy Polenta Bites:**

Turn polenta into delightful bites with a crispy exterior and a soft, creamy interior.

- **Mediterranean Mezze Platter:**

Assemble a colorful mezze platter with an assortment of small plates, including olives, feta, and stuffed grape leaves.

- **Sweet Potato Tots:**

Experience the sweet and crispy joy of sweet potato tots, perfect as a snack or side.

- **Spinach and Artichoke Dip Stuffed Peppers:**

Combine the flavors of spinach and artichoke dip with sweet bell peppers for a delectable small plate.

Whether you're hosting a party, looking for a quick snack, or seeking the perfect complement to your main course, these sides and small plates offer a variety of delicious options. Let your air fryer take the lead in creating these delightful additions to your meals.

AIR FRYER BAKING: CAKES, PASTRIES, AND MORE

This chapter explores the world of baking in your air fryer, showcasing the versatility of this appliance when it comes to creating delectable cakes, pastries, and other baked goods. From light and fluffy cakes to golden pastries, you'll be amazed at the sweet treats you can create with your air fryer.

- **Moist Chocolate Cake:**

Bake a rich and moist chocolate cake with a velvety texture, perfect for any chocolate lover.

- **Blueberry Muffins:**

Prepare tender and fruity blueberry muffins with a golden crumb topping.

- **Apple Turnovers:**

Bake flaky apple turnovers filled with warm, cinnamon-spiced apple filling.

- **Lemon Drizzle Pound Cake:**

Create a zesty and moist pound cake with a lemony drizzle that's bursting with flavor.

- **Cherry Hand Pies:**

Make handheld cherry pies with a buttery crust and a sweet cherry filling.

- **Cinnamon Rolls with Cream Cheese Glaze:**

Indulge in cinnamon rolls with a gooey cinnamon swirl and a decadent cream cheese glaze.

- **Almond Croissants:**

Bake almond croissants with a crispy exterior and a sweet, nutty filling.

- **Red Velvet Cupcakes:**

Prepare classic red velvet cupcakes with a luscious cream cheese frosting.

- **Raspberry Danish:**

Create flaky and fruity raspberry danishes that make a delightful breakfast or dessert.

- **Vanilla Eclairs:**

Craft vanilla eclairs filled with a creamy vanilla pastry cream and a glossy chocolate glaze.

- **Coffee Cake:**

Bake a moist coffee cake with a crumbly streusel topping that pairs perfectly with your morning brew.

- **Nutella-Stuffed Donuts:**

Whip up donuts filled with luscious Nutella, topped with a dusting of powdered sugar.

- **Strawberry Shortcake:**

Enjoy light and fluffy strawberry shortcakes with sweet, ripe strawberries and whipped cream.

- **Cheese Danish:**

Create flaky cheese danishes filled with a creamy and sweet cheese filling.

- **Mini Apple Cider Donuts:**

Bake miniature donuts with the warm and comforting flavor of apple cider.

Air fryer baking is not only convenient but also allows for quick and even cooking, resulting in scrumptious baked goods that you and your loved ones will adore. Get ready to satisfy your sweet tooth with these cakes, pastries, and more, all prepared in your air fryer.

SALADS WITH A CRUNCH

In this chapter, we're going to reimagine salads by adding a delightful element of crunch. These salad recipes are all about texture and flavor, combining crisp, fresh vegetables with various toppings and dressings to create mouthwatering and satisfying salads.

- **Crispy Chicken Caesar Salad:**

Elevate your Caesar salad with air-fried crispy chicken tenders and homemade Caesar dressing.

- **Asian-Inspired Crunchy Coleslaw:**

Prepare a refreshing coleslaw with a variety of colorful veggies and a sesame ginger dressing.

- **Caprese Salad with Crispy Prosciutto:**

Combine the classic Caprese flavors of tomatoes, mozzarella, and basil with crispy prosciutto for a delightful twist.

- **Roasted Chickpea and Avocado Salad:**

Create a satisfying salad with roasted chickpeas, ripe avocado, and a tangy vinaigrette.

- **Taco Salad with Crunchy Tortilla Strips:**

Build a Tex-Mex-inspired salad with seasoned ground beef, fresh veggies, and crispy tortilla strips.

- **Grilled Halloumi Salad:**

Experience the unique texture and flavor of grilled halloumi cheese paired with fresh greens and a lemon dressing.

- **Asian Crunchy Noodle Salad:**

Whip up a vibrant salad with crisp vegetables, toasted almonds, and crunchy ramen noodles, all tossed in a soy-based dressing.

- **Quinoa and Chickpea Crunch Salad:**

Combine quinoa, chickpeas, and a variety of veggies for a protein-packed and crunchy salad.

- **Greek Salad with Pita Chips:**

Create a Greek-inspired salad with ripe tomatoes, cucumbers, feta cheese, and homemade pita chips for added crunch.

- **Waldorf Salad with Candied Walnuts:**

Prepare a classic Waldorf salad featuring crisp apples, celery, and candied walnuts.

- **Barbecue Ranch Chopped Salad:**

Whip up a barbecue-inspired salad with grilled chicken, corn, and a creamy ranch dressing.

- **Spicy Cucumber and Peanut Salad:**

Savor the refreshing combination of cucumbers, peanuts, and a spicy dressing for a lively crunch.

- **Mediterranean Chickpea Salad with Feta:**

Craft a Mediterranean-inspired salad with chickpeas, feta cheese, olives, and a lemon vinaigrette.

- **Southwest Black Bean and Corn Salad:**

Prepare a colorful salad with black beans, corn, and a zesty southwestern dressing.

- **Crispy Bacon and Potato Salad:**

Indulge in a hearty potato salad with crispy bacon, green onions, and a creamy dressing.

These salads are designed to provide a satisfying crunch that complements the freshness of the vegetables and the richness of various toppings and dressings. Enjoy the textures and flavors of these salads with a crunch for a truly delightful meal.

GLOBAL FLAVORS: AIR-FRIED INTERNATIONAL CUISINE

In this chapter, we embark on a culinary journey around the world, exploring a diverse range of international dishes that can be prepared with the magic of your air fryer. From spicy Indian curries to savory Italian pasta, these recipes bring global flavors to your kitchen, no passport required.

- **Tandoori Chicken:**

Experience the bold and aromatic spices of Indian cuisine with air-fried tandoori chicken.

- **Thai Basil Stir-Fry:**

Whip up a spicy and fragrant Thai basil stir-fry, featuring your choice of protein and fresh herbs.

- **Japanese Gyoza Dumplings:**

Prepare delicate and crispy gyoza dumplings filled with a delectable mixture of meats and vegetables.

- **Mexican Street Corn (Elote):**

Enjoy the zesty flavors of Mexican street corn, or elote, with a smoky and creamy topping.

- **Spanish Patatas Bravas:**

Indulge in Spanish patatas bravas—crispy potatoes served with a spicy tomato sauce and aioli.

- **Moroccan Spiced Lamb Kebabs:**

Experience the rich and aromatic spices of Morocco with air-fried lamb kebabs.

- **Chinese Orange Chicken:**

Create a sweet and tangy Chinese orange chicken with crispy nuggets of chicken and a luscious sauce.

- **Italian Eggplant Parmesan:**

Prepare the classic Italian dish of eggplant Parmesan, featuring layers of crispy eggplant and melty cheese.

- **Brazilian Feijoada:**

Experience the hearty and flavorful Brazilian feijoada—black bean stew with various cuts of pork.

- **Korean Bibimbap:**

Craft a vibrant Korean bibimbap bowl with rice, marinated vegetables, and your choice of protein, all topped with a fried egg.

- **French Croque Monsieur:**

Whip up a delicious French croque monsieur—a toasted ham and cheese sandwich with a creamy béchamel sauce.

- **Greek Spanakopita:**

Indulge in Greek spanakopita, a savory pastry filled with spinach, feta, and herbs.

- **Lebanese Falafel:**

Create crispy and spiced Lebanese falafel, perfect for stuffing into pita bread with tahini sauce.

- **Vietnamese Spring Rolls:**

Prepare fresh and flavorful Vietnamese spring rolls, filled with shrimp, herbs, and vermicelli noodles.

- **Peruvian Lomo Saltado:**

Savor the fusion of Chinese and Peruvian flavors with lomo saltado—a stir-fry of beef, tomatoes, and onions served with French fries.

These global flavors come to life in your air fryer, allowing you to explore the world of international cuisine without leaving your kitchen. Whether you're a fan of spicy curries or savory pasta dishes, you'll find a variety of dishes to satisfy your global cravings.

HEALTHY EATING ON A BUDGET

This chapter is all about embracing a nutritious and balanced diet without breaking the bank. You'll discover practical and budget-friendly recipes that focus on whole, affordable ingredients, helping you maintain your health and save money at the same time.

- **Budget-Friendly Veggie Stir-Fry:**

Create a colorful stir-fry with an assortment of affordable vegetables and tofu or chicken, all served over rice.

- **Lentil and Vegetable Soup:**

Whip up a hearty lentil and vegetable soup that's both filling and budget-conscious.

- **Rice and Beans with Salsa:**

Enjoy a simple yet satisfying combination of rice, beans, and salsa for a quick and affordable meal.

- **Affordable Pasta Primavera:**

Prepare a pasta primavera with seasonal and budget-friendly vegetables, tossed in a light olive oil and herb dressing.

- **Baked Sweet Potatoes with Black Beans:**

Roast sweet potatoes and top them with black beans, salsa, and a dollop of yogurt for a budget-friendly and nutritious dish.

- **Budget-Friendly Chickpea Curry:**

Experience the flavors of an Indian-inspired chickpea curry made with affordable pantry staples.

- **Tuna and White Bean Salad:**

Create a protein-packed salad with canned tuna and white beans, mixed with budget-friendly veggies and a lemon vinaigrette.

- **Budget-Friendly Oatmeal:**

Start your day with a wholesome bowl of budget-friendly oatmeal, topped with fruits and nuts.

- **Potato and Egg Breakfast Hash:**

Prepare a hearty breakfast hash with potatoes, eggs, and budget-friendly vegetables, perfect for a filling morning meal.

- **Homemade Bean Burritos:**

Roll up homemade bean burritos filled with affordable ingredients like beans, rice, and veggies.

- **Budget-Friendly Greek Salad:**

Whip up a Greek salad with budget-friendly ingredients like cucumbers, tomatoes, olives, and feta cheese, all drizzled with olive oil and lemon juice.

- **Budget-Friendly Quinoa Bowl:**

Create a quinoa bowl with budget-friendly toppings like roasted vegetables, chickpeas, and a tahini drizzle.

- **Budget-Friendly Veggie Frittata:**

Bake a delicious veggie frittata using budget-friendly vegetables, eggs, and a touch of cheese.

- **Budget-Friendly Minestrone Soup:**

Simmer a pot of budget-friendly minestrone soup packed with pasta, beans, and affordable vegetables.

- **DIY Budget-Friendly Pizza:**

Craft your own pizza with a budget-friendly homemade crust and your favorite toppings.

30-MINUTE MEALS WITH YOUR AIR FRYER

This chapter is dedicated to the busy days when you need a quick and delicious meal in no time. You'll find a collection of recipes that can be prepared in just 30 minutes or less using your trusty air fryer. Say goodbye to long cooking times and hello to fast and flavorful dishes.

- **Quick Air-Fried Chicken Tenders:**

Whip up crispy chicken tenders in no time, perfect for a speedy and satisfying meal.

- **Speedy Shrimp Scampi:**

Prepare a zesty shrimp scampi with garlic, butter, and a hint of lemon for a quick seafood delight.

- **Fast and Flavorful Stir-Fry:**

Create a stir-fry with your choice of protein and colorful vegetables, all tossed in a savory sauce.

- **30-Minute Beef and Broccoli:**

Whip up a classic beef and broccoli stir-fry that's ready to enjoy in half an hour.

- **Speedy Veggie Quesadillas:**

Craft veggie quesadillas filled with sautéed vegetables and cheese for a quick and cheesy treat.

- **Quick and Easy BLT Sandwich:**

Make a classic BLT sandwich with crispy bacon, fresh lettuce, and juicy tomatoes.k

- **Speedy Margherita Pizza:**

Create a Margherita pizza with fresh basil, mozzarella, and a crispy crust in just 30 minutes.

- **Fast and Healthy Chicken Salad:**

Prepare a nutritious and quick chicken salad with your choice of greens and a flavorful dressing.

- **Speedy Lemon Garlic Shrimp Pasta:**

Whip up a delightful lemon garlic shrimp pasta in no time for a satisfying and zesty meal.

- **30-Minute Veggie Tacos:**

Craft flavorful vegetarian tacos filled with beans, sautéed veggies, and your favorite toppings.

- **Quick and Spicy Black Bean Soup:**

Simmer a spicy black bean soup that's rich in flavor and ready to serve in 30 minutes.

- **Speedy Teriyaki Salmon:**

Bake teriyaki-glazed salmon fillets in your air fryer for a quick and delicious seafood dish.

- **Fast and Fresh Caprese Salad:**

Assemble a Caprese salad with ripe tomatoes, mozzarella, basil, and balsamic glaze in mere minutes.

- **Quick Breakfast Burritos:**

Create breakfast burritos filled with scrambled eggs, cheese, and your favorite morning fixings.

- **Speedy Veggie Pad Thai:**

Prepare a veggie-packed Pad Thai with your choice of protein for a flavorful and quick meal.

These 30-minute meals are designed to save you time in the kitchen without compromising on flavor. With your air fryer, you can have a tasty and satisfying meal on the table in no time, making busy weeknight dinners a breeze.

LOW-CARB AND KETO-FRIENDLY OPTIONS

In this chapter, you'll find a collection of recipes tailored to those following a low-carb or keto lifestyle. These dishes are designed to keep your carb intake in check while delivering flavor and satisfaction.

- **Keto-Friendly Chicken Alfredo:**

Indulge in a creamy and low-carb chicken Alfredo with zucchini noodles.

- **Low-Carb Cauliflower Pizza:**

Create a delicious and low-carb pizza crust made from cauliflower, topped with your favorite keto-friendly toppings.

- **Keto Taco Salad:**

Enjoy a taco salad with seasoned ground beef, lettuce, cheese, and a creamy keto-friendly dressing.

- **Zucchini Noodles with Pesto:**

Savor zucchini noodles with a vibrant pesto sauce for a low-carb alternative to traditional pasta.

- **Low-Carb Beef and Broccoli Stir-Fry:**

Prepare a low-carb beef and broccoli stir-fry that's big on flavor and low on carbs.

- **Keto-Friendly Spaghetti Squash Carbonara:**

Create a keto-friendly version of spaghetti carbonara using roasted spaghetti squash.

- **Low-Carb Stuffed Bell Peppers:**

Make stuffed bell peppers with a low-carb filling that's both delicious and nutritious.

- **Keto-Friendly Avocado and Bacon Salad:**

Indulge in an avocado and bacon salad that's rich in healthy fats and flavor.

- **Low-Carb Cauliflower Rice Bowls:**

Craft cauliflower rice bowls with your choice of protein and an array of low-carb toppings.

- **Keto-Friendly Salmon with Asparagus:**

Bake salmon with asparagus and a lemon herb butter for a keto-friendly and flavorful meal.

- **Low-Carb Eggplant Parmesan:**

Prepare a low-carb version of eggplant Parmesan with crispy slices and a savory sauce.

- **Keto Broccoli and Cheddar Soup:**

Simmer a creamy and keto-friendly broccoli and cheddar soup, perfect for a low-carb lunch.

- **Low-Carb Beef and Cabbage Stir-Fry:**

Whip up a low-carb beef and cabbage stir-fry that's quick, easy, and satisfying.

- **Keto-Friendly Greek Salad:**

Create a keto-friendly Greek salad with fresh veggies, olives, feta cheese, and a flavorful dressing.

- **Low-Carb and Keto-Friendly Cheesecake:**

Indulge in a creamy and keto-friendly cheesecake with a nut-based crust, perfect for a low-carb dessert.

These low-carb and keto-friendly recipes are tailored to your dietary preferences while ensuring you can enjoy flavorful and satisfying meals that align with your low-carb lifestyle. Whether you're looking for dinner options or a sweet treat, these recipes have you covered.

AIR FRYER TIPS AKND TRICKS

In this chapter, we'll explore a collection of valuable tips and tricks to help you make the most of your air fryer. Whether you're a beginner or an experienced user, these insights will enhance your air frying experience and ensure your dishes come out perfectly every time.

- **Preheat Your Air Fryer:**

Preheating your air fryer for a few minutes before cooking helps ensure even cooking and crisp results.

- **Use Oil Wisely:**

Use a mister or oil spray to lightly coat your ingredients with oil for that crispy finish, rather than submerging them.

- **Arrange Food in a Single Layer:**

Avoid overcrowding the air fryer basket to allow proper air circulation, which is crucial for even cooking.

- **Shake or Flip Food:**

For even cooking, remember to shake or flip your food halfway through the cooking time.

- **Invest in a Meat Thermometer:**

A meat thermometer is your best friend for perfectly cooked proteins; it helps you avoid overcooking or undercooking.

- **Experiment with Seasonings:**

Don't be afraid to experiment with various seasonings and spices to add flavor to your dishes.

- **Use Parchment Paper:**

Parchment paper can help prevent food from sticking to the basket and makes cleanup easier.

- **Monitor Cooking Time:**

Keep a close eye on your food, especially the first few times you use your air fryer, to prevent overcooking.

- **Get Creative with Breading:**

Experiment with different types of coatings like panko, almond flour, or coconut for various textures.

- **Precook or Par-Cook Ingredients:**

For certain foods like potatoes, precooking or par-cooking can help ensure they're fully cooked and crispy.

- **Make Your Own Marinades:**

Creating your own marinades and sauces allows you to customize flavors to your liking.

- **Invest in Accessories:**

Explore air fryer accessories like grill pans, racks, and silicone molds to expand your cooking options.

- **Keep the Air Fryer Clean:**

Regularly clean the basket and the interior of your air fryer to prevent residue buildup.

- **Adjust Temperature and Time:**

Feel free to adjust cooking temperature and time to suit your preferences and your air fryer's specific performance.

- **Record Your Successes:**

Keep a record of successful recipes, times, and temperatures to replicate your favorite dishes easily.

These air fryer tips and tricks are here to enhance your cooking experience, making your time in the kitchen more enjoyable and your results consistently satisfying. Whether you're a novice or a pro, you'll find these insights invaluable for your air frying adventures.

ENTERTAINING WITH YOUR AIR FRYER

Entertaining guests is a breeze with your air fryer. This chapter is dedicated to showing you how to create an impressive spread of appetizers, snacks, and main courses that will delight your guests while making hosting a stress-free experience.

- **Air-Fried Party Wings:**

Serve up a platter of crispy and flavorful chicken winkgs with various sauces for dipping.

- **Spinach and Artichoke Dip Stuffed Mushrooms:**

Impress your guests with stuffed mushrooms filled with a creamy spinach and artichoke dip.

- **Mini Sliders with Air-Fried Fries:**

Create bite-sized sliders served with perfectly crispy air-fried fries.

- **Air-Fried Mozzarella Sticks:**

Offer a classic appetizer with mozzarella sticks that are gooey on the inside and crispy on the outside.

- **Loaded Nachos:**

Prepare a mountain of loaded nachos with all your favorite toppings, baked to perfection in your air fryer.

- **Bacon-Wrapped Dates:**

Indulge in the sweet and savory combination of bacon-wrapped dates, a delightful appetizer.

- **Air-Fried Shrimp Cocktail:**

Serve succulent shrimp with cocktail sauce, all perfectly air-fried for a quick and elegant appetizer.

- **Air-Fried Spring Rolls:**

Make crispy spring rolls filled with a variety of ingredients and accompanied by dipping sauces.

- **Stuffed Peppers:**

Create a colorful and delicious appetizer by filling sweet bell peppers with your choice of stuffing.

- **Beef Tenderloin with Garlic Butter:**

Impress your guests with a perfectly cooked beef tenderloin, drizzled with garlic butter.

- **Vegetarian Mezze Platter:**

Assemble a colorful mezze platter with an assortment of small plates, including hummus, falafel, olives, and more.

- **Air-Fried Coconut Shrimp:**

Offer a taste of the tropics with air-fried coconut shrimp, complete with a sweet dipping sauce.

- **Baked Brie with Cranberry Sauce:**

Serve a warm and gooey baked Brie with cranberry sauce and crackers for an elegant appetizer.

- **Air-Fried Tacos:**

Let your guests build their own tacos with various toppings and proteins, all cooked to perfection in the air fryer.

- **Mini Air-Fried Desserts:**

End the meal with a variety of miniature air-fried desserts like mini donuts, churros, or apple turnovers.

Entertaining with your air fryer allows you to impress your guests with a variety of delicious dishes while making your hosting duties more manageable. These recipes are perfect for gatherings, parties, or any occasion where good food and good company come together.

FAMILY-FRIENDLY FAVORITES

Entertaining guests is a breeze with your air fryer. This chapter is dedicated to showing you how to create an impressive spread of appetizers, snacks, and main courses that will delight your guests while making hosting a stress-free experience.

- **Air-Fried Party Wings:**

Serve up a platter of crispy and flavorful chicken wings with various sauces for dipping.

- **Spinach and Artichoke Dip Stuffed Mushrooms:**

Impress your guests with stuffed mushrooms filled with a creamy spinach and artichoke dip.

- **Mini Sliders with Air-Fried Fries:**

Create bite-sized sliders served with perfectly crispy air-fried fries.

- **Air-Fried Mozzarella Sticks:**

Offer a classic appetizer with mozzarella sticks that are gooey on the inside and crispy on the outside.

- **Loaded Nachos:**

Prepare a mountain of loaded nachos with all your favorite toppings, baked to perfection in your air fryer.

- **Bacon-Wrapped Dates:**

Indulge in the sweet and savory combination of bacon-wrapped dates, a delightful appetizer.

- **Air-Fried Shrimp Cocktail:**

Serve succulent shrimp with cocktail sauce, all perfectly air-fried for a quick and elegant appetizer.

- **Air-Fried Spring Rolls:**

Make crispy spring rolls filled with a variety of ingredients and accompanied by dipping sauces.

- **Stuffed Peppers:**

Create a colorful and delicious appetizer by filling sweet bell peppers with your choice of stuffing.

- **Beef Tenderloin with Garlic Butter:**

Impress your guests with a perfectly cooked beef tenderloin, drizzled with garlic butter.

- **Vegetarian Mezze Platter:**

Assemble a colorful mezze platter with an assortment of small plates, including hummus, falafel, olives, and more.

- **Air-Fried Coconut Shrimp:**

Offer a taste of the tropics with air-fried coconut shrimp, complete with a sweet dipping sauce.

- **Baked Brie with Cranberry Sauce:**

Serve a warm and gooey baked Brie with kcranberry sauce and crackers for an elegant appetizer.

- **Air-Fried Tacos:**

Let your guests build their own tacos with various toppings and proteins, all cooked to perfection in the air fryer.

- **Mini Air-Fried Desserts:**

End the meal with a variety of miniature air-fried desserts like mini donuts, churros, or apple turnovers.

Entertaining with your air fryer allows you to impress your guests with a variety of delicious dishes while making your hosting duties more manageable. These recipes are perfect for gatherings, parties, or any occasion where good food and good company come together.

SWEET ENDINGS: DELECTABLE DESSERT CREATIONS

This chapter is dedicated to indulgent and delectable dessert creations that will satisfy your sweet tooth and leave a lasting impression. From classic treats to unique creations, these dessert recipes are perfect for any occasion.

- **Molten Chocolate Lava Cakes:**

Prepare warm and gooey chocolate lava cakes that reveal a molten center when you dig in.

- **Air-Fried Donuts:**

Indulge in homemade donuts that are light, fluffy, and perfectly air-fried to a golden brown.

- **Decadent Chocolate Fondue:**

Create a luxurious chocolate fondue for dipping a variety of fruits, marshmallows, and treats.

- **Apple Cinnamon Dumplings:**

Bake apple cinnamon dumplings that are like little pockets of apple pie goodness.

- **Air-Fried Cheesecake:**

Enjoy creamy cheesecake with a crispy crust, all air-fried to perfection.

- **Crispy Churros:**

Make churros that are crisp on the outside and soft on the inside, perfect for dipping in chocolate sauce.

- **Fruit Hand Pies:**

Prepare mini fruit hand pies filled with your favorite fruits and a flaky crust.

- **Air-Fried S'mores:**

Recreate the campfire classic with air-fried s'mores that are perfectly toasted and gooey.

- **Lemon Bars:**

Whip up zesty and sweet lemon bars with a buttery crust and a tart lemon filling.

- **Nutella-Stuffed Crescent Rolls:**

Create sweet crescent rolls filled with Nutella and baked to perfection.

- **Air-Fried Cinnamon Sugar Donut Holes:**

Indulge in bite-sized donut holes, air-fried and coated in cinnamon sugar.

- **Mini Cheesecake Bites:**

Prepare mini cheesecake bites with various toppings and flavors for a delightful dessert platter.

- **Chocolate-Dipped Strawberries:**

Enjoy the classic combination of ripe strawberries dipped in rich dark chocolate.

- **Air-Fried Brownie Bites:**

Bake bite-sized brownie treats that are fudgy, moist, and utterly irresistible.

- **Pecan Pie Tarts:**

Create miniature pecan pie tarts that are the perfect balance of nutty and sweet.

These dessert creations are meant to provide a sweet ending to any meal or occasion. Whether you're looking for a classic treat or a unique dessert experience, these recipes are sure to delight your taste buds and those of your loved ones.